Investigate

Animal Needs

Sue Barraclough

Heinemann Library is an imprint of Pearson Education Limited,
a company incorporated in England and Wales having its
registered office at Edinburgh Gate, Harlow, Essex, CM20 2JE
– Registered company number: 00872828

Heinemann is a registered trademark of Pearson Education Ltd.
Text © Pearson Education Limited 2008
First published in hardback in 2008
Paperback edition first published in 2009
The moral rights of the proprietor have been asserted.

Edited by Sarah Shannon, Catherine Clarke, and Laura Knowles
Designed by Joanna Hinton-Malivoire, Victoria Bevan,
  and Hart McLeod
Picture research by Liz Alexander
Production by Duncan Gilbert
Originated by Chroma Graphics (Overseas) Pte. Ltd
Printed and bound in China by Leo Paper Group

ISBN 978 0 431932 73 6 (hardback)
12 11 10 09 08
10 9 8 7 6 5 4 3 2 1

ISBN 978 0 431932 92 7 (paperback)
13 12 11 10 09
10 9 8 7 6 5 4 3 2 1

British Library Cataloguing in Publication Data
Barraclough, Sue
  Animal needs. - (Investigate)
  591
BA full catalogue record for this book is available from the
British Library.

Acknowledgements
We would like to thank the following for permission to reproduce
photographs: ©Alamy pp. **6** (D. Hurst), **8** (Papilio), **11** (Keren
Su/China Span), **14** (Robert Harding Picture Library Ltd.), **17**
(Dave Watts), **21** (Craig Lovell/Eagle Visions Photography), **24**
(Mediacolour's), **26** (blickwinkel), **27** (Amazon-Images); ©Corbis
pp. **10** (Frank Lucasseck), **13** (Tom Brakefield), **16** (DLILLC), **25**
(Kennan Ward); ©Digital Vision p. **22**; ©FLPA pp. **7** (Winfried
Wisniewski), **9** (Flip Nicklin/Minden Pictures), **12** (Colin Elsey),
19 (Frans Lanting), **20** (Nigel Cattlin), **23** (Edwin Giesbers/FOTO
NATURA); ©istockphoto p. **15** (Iztok Grilc); ©NHPA/Stephen
Dalton p. **18**; ©Photolibrary pp. **4** (Oxford Scientific/Ariadne Van
Zandbergen), **5** (Oxford Scientific (OSF)/Richard Packwood).

Cover photograph of Red Squirrel (Sciurus vulgaris) feeding,
Northumberland, UK, reproduced with permission of ©NaturePL
(Roger Powell).

Every effort has been made to contact copyright holders of
material reproduced in this book. Any omissions will be rectified in
subsequent printings if notice is given to the publishers.

Contents

Some words are shown in bold, **like this**. You can find out what they mean by looking in the glossary.

Animal needs

All animals need certain things to live.
All animals need:

- ⟹ air
- ⟹ food
- ⟹ water
- ⟹ shelter.

Animals have different ways to meet their needs.
Their bodies have parts to help them to breathe,
and to get water and food.

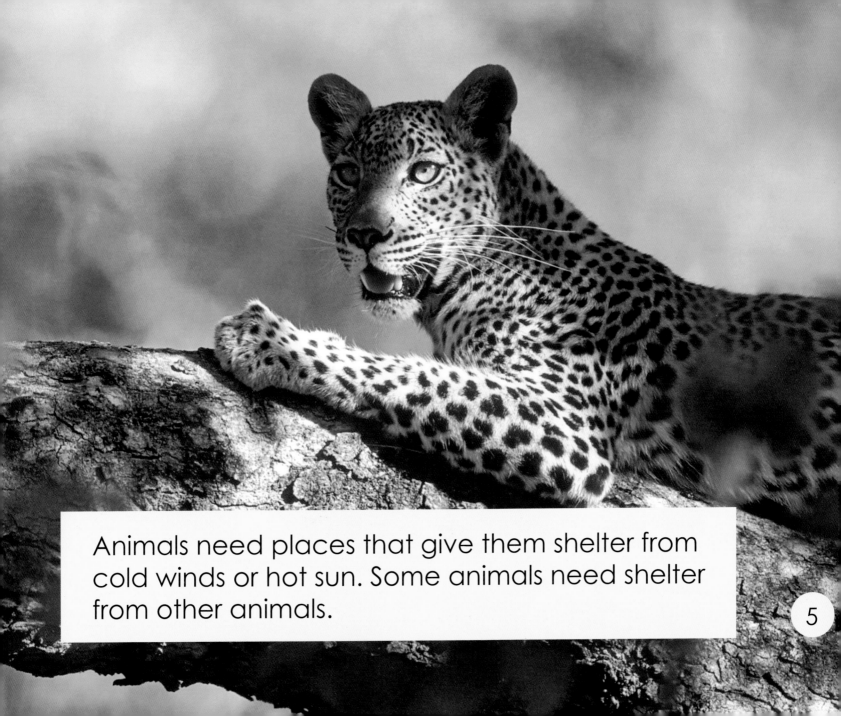

Animals need places that give them shelter from cold winds or hot sun. Some animals need shelter from other animals.

5

Animals need air

Animals need **oxygen** from the air. Oxygen is a **gas** in air and water. Animals have different ways to take in oxygen. Many animals that live on land have **lungs** to help them breathe.

This cow breathes in air through its nose.

Some animals live in water.

Q How do fish breathe?

CLUE
- Where do fish live?

Fish use **gills** to take in oxygen from water.

gill

8 Many animals, such as fish, can take in oxygen from water.

Some animals live in water but they need oxygen from the air. Whales and seals have lungs. They need to swim up to the surface to breathe oxygen.

Animals need food

Animals need to eat food. Food helps them to keep warm, move, and grow. Many animals eat plant parts such as leaves, seeds, nuts, and roots.

⬆ This panda eats bamboo leaves.

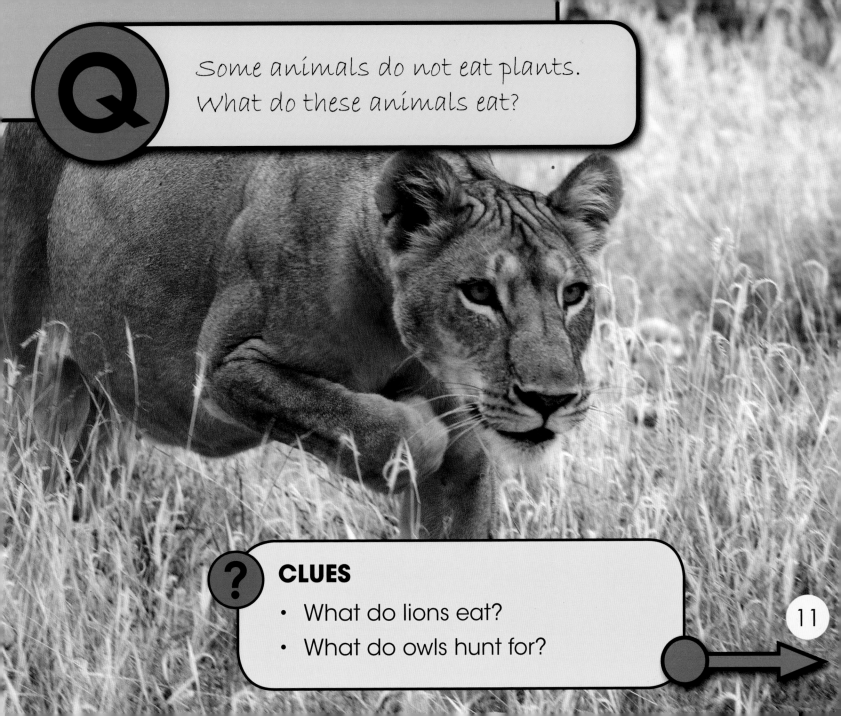

Q Some animals do not eat plants. What do these animals eat?

? CLUES

- What do lions eat?
- What do owls hunt for?

11

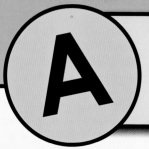**A**

Some animals eat other animals.
These animals are called **predators**.

12

 These lions have caught an antelope to eat.

An anteater looks for ants to eat. It scoops up the ants with its long tongue.

Monkeys are good climbers. They use their long arms and strong tails to climb trees to find food to eat.

Q How do giraffes use their long necks?

CLUE

- Giraffes eat leaves from trees.

A Giraffes use their long necks to reach leaves on tall trees.

16

Birds often have beaks that are shaped to help them eat. Some birds have long, sharp beaks to spear fish. Some birds have small, strong beaks for cracking seeds.

⬆ A hummingbird has a long, thin beak to reach **nectar** in flowers.

Animals need water

All animals need water to live. Most animals go to lakes or rivers to drink water. This swallow flies down to drink from a lake.

These animals come to a waterhole to drink.
Elephants drink water by sucking it up their trunks.

Q Do all animals drink water?

? CLUE
• Do fish drink?

A Not all animals drink water.

Many animals do not drink water. This is because they get water from the plants they eat. Snails eat leaves that have water in them. This means that they do not need to drink water.

Many insects, such as bees, drink **nectar** so they do not need to drink water. Fish do not need to drink water. They live in water and they take it in through their skin and **gills**.

Animals need shelter

Animals need shelter from the weather and from other animals. Some animals have thick fur or hard **scales** to protect them from cold or heat. Some animals have spikes or hard shells to protect them from other animals.

A tortoise's shell provides shelter from the weather and protection from other animals.

Some animals dig **burrows** under the ground. A burrow shelters them from cold winds, hot sun, or **predators**.

 Why do birds build nests?

A Nests are safe places to lay eggs and look after baby birds.

Birds often build nests in trees. This means that they are safe from other animals.

Polar bears dig **dens** in the snow and ice. This makes a warm, safe place to rear their young.

↑ These three polar bear cubs are coming out of their den for the first time.

Many animals live in big groups. Zebras live in big groups called **herds**. This means that some zebras can drink or feed while the others look out for danger.

Ants live in big groups called colonies. They build huge nests to live in. They work together to find food.

A place to live

Animals live in many different places all over the world. All animals live in places that have the things they need: food, water, air, and shelter.

 Rainforests are warm and wet with plenty of food and so lots of animals live there.

 Deserts are very dry because hardly any rain falls there. Only certain animals can survive there.

 Cold, rocky places have few plants so there is less food for animals to eat.

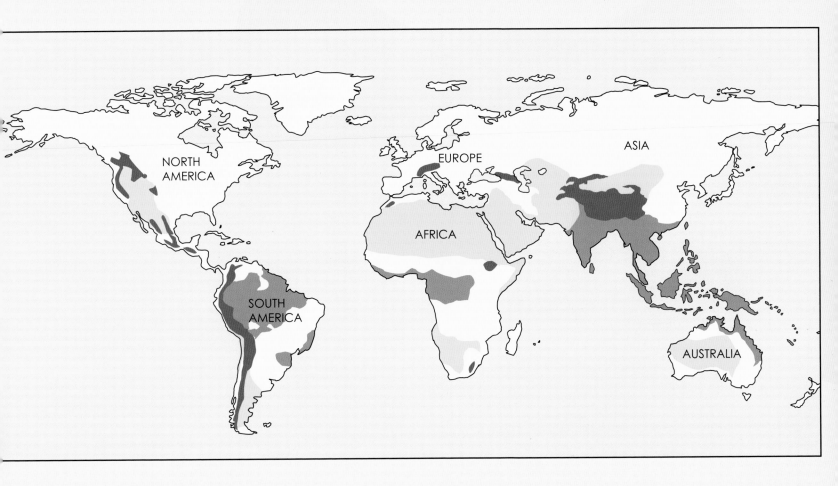

NORTH
AMERICA

EUROPE

ASIA

AFRICA

SOUTH
AMERICA

AUSTRALIA

29

Checklist

Animals need:

➡ air

➡ food

➡ water

➡ shelter.

Animals live in places that give them the things they need.

Glossary

burrow hole or tunnel in the ground. Animals such as rabbits dig burrows to live in.

den animal home

gas air-like substance that we cannot see. The air around us is a mixture of gases.

gill part of a fish's body that it uses to breathe. Gills take oxygen out of water.

herd group of animals

lung part of an animal's body that is used for breathing. People have two lungs.

nectar sweet liquid found in flowers. Insects and some birds drink nectar.

oxygen gas found in air and water. Animals need oxygen to breathe.

predator animal that feeds on other animals

scale small plate on an animal's body. Animals with scales have them all over their body instead of skin or fur.

Index